AMERICAN HOME

SEAN CHO A.

AMERICAN HOME

An Autumn House Book

Typeset in Minion Pro
Cover design by Kinsley Stocum
Cover art sources:
Wrapping Cloth, Pojagi. *Made 1801–1900, Silk, plain weave; pieced; attached ribbon and cord. Art Institute of Chicago, Chicago.*
Printed in the USA

ISBN: 978-1-63768-008-7

All Autumn House books are printed on acid-free paper and meet the international standards of permanent books intended for purchase by libraries.

Autumn House Press receives state arts funding support through a grant from the Pennsylvania Council on the Arts, a state agency funded by the Commonwealth of Pennsylvania, and the National Endowment for the Arts, a federal agency.

www.autumnhouse.org

SEAN CHO A.

AMERICAN HOME

Table of Contents

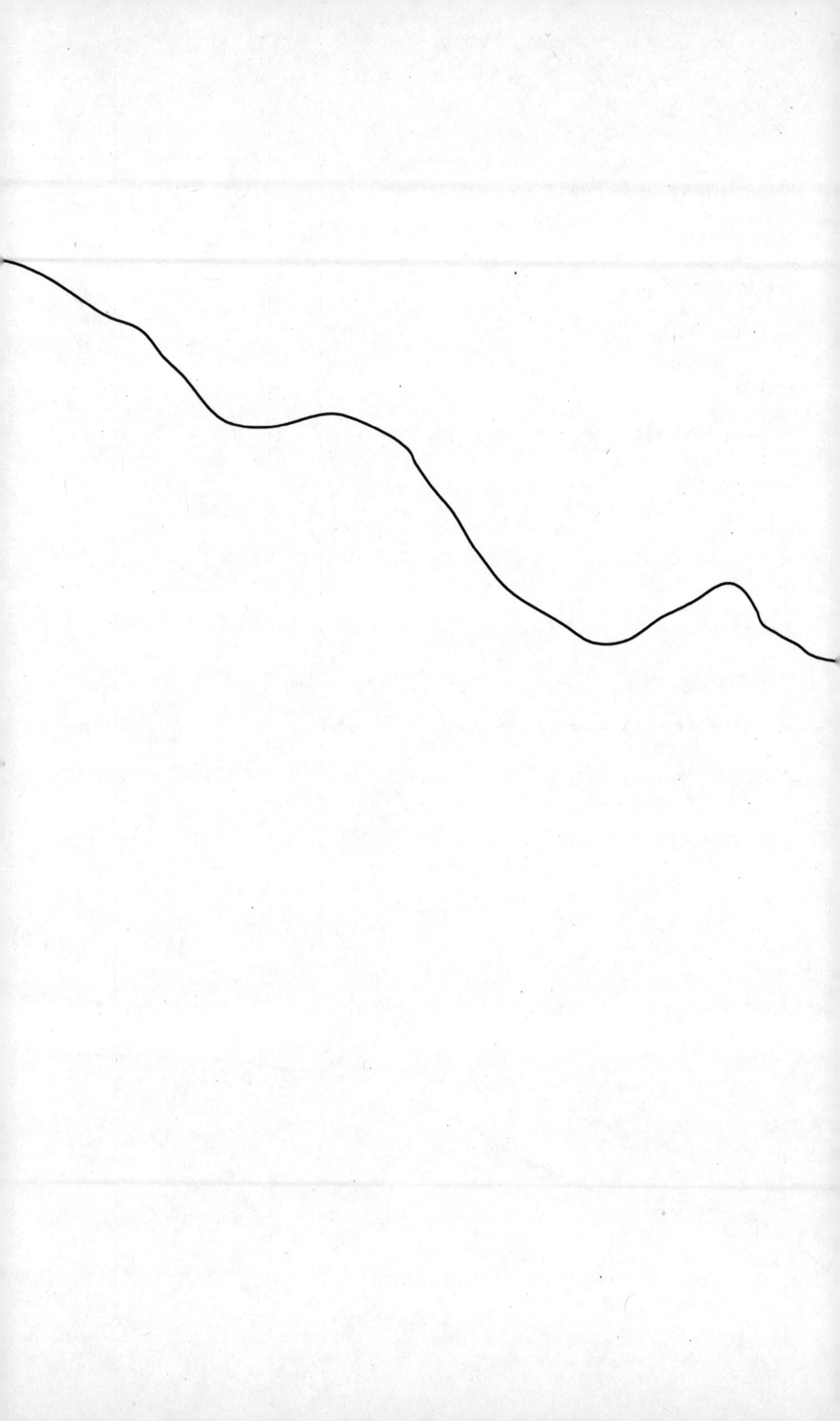

AMERICAN HOME

Desire/Excellence

I came to America too young
to be foreign, so all my dreams
are American and contemporary,
present and blinding as morning-hunger:
a fat gull scavenges for loose plastic bags
and their crumb-treasures
on the winter sand. On the television,
a well-dressed man (who, back home, people
would ask if he was my brother) thanks the University
for his success. All while I'm stealing one too many
week-old sandwiches from the food pantry.
Look, the tangelos are losing
their green. I won't apologize for the smallness
of my delights.

September Children/Faith Production

I

Cold winter with idle time.

II

Fresh life. Say the trees
are sick. Say God
is God. Say the ground
is loathsome and lifeless.

III

Leaf piles like little
altars. A clean lawn:
a sign of devotion.

IV

The snow pears are coated
in icelike jewels.
Prayer is explained
to a child as the good
kind of want.

V

I remember waking
in March. Our yard
was full of violets:
white-purple and
white and purple.

When I ask you to tell me what I dreamed last night

"The payphone rings. You pick it up. We can now assume this is a dream. It's windy and just hot enough for you to take off your shirt. So you do. You almost have a six-pack. You love your body. This is a dream, so why not? All of this is about want. The man on your ear sounds a lot like your father or the man whose house you snuck out of last night, boxers in hand, clumsy and unsatisfied. He says, *come back*. You hang up the phone because you can. After all, this is your dream. There's blood on the phone cord. You notice blood on your hand. You search your body for a wound: chest fine, arms fine, legs fine. You become preoccupied with the fineness of the body. Context matters. In this situation, *fine* does not mean wound-free. It's the years of waking early, choking on raw yolks, throwing rusty free weights over your head, dry-chicken-breast-for-every-dinner kind of fine. There's a bird at your feet. You pick up the limp body. Wipe your hand-blood into its open beak, toss him in the air, and he flies away. *Look at you, little saint!* The phone rings again, reminder: none of this is real. So you pick up the phone, *are you leaving yet?* This time, it's cold. This time, you're wearing a blue sweater, one red mitten, one white mitten. Logic would lead you to assume that your hand is bleeding. But you don't want logic. Logic is boring. Logic is that 2 percent bank interest, but you want scratch cards. You want to take a week's worth of pocket change, slam it on the gas station countertop demanding luck. Then scrape the ridges of laundry quarters against silver cardboard and reveal filthy delight, ten more ugly could-be-surprises worth of delights. It's a cycle. The phone rings, but you don't want to answer. You know he will be yelling, impatiently yelling—so you don't. You can't. This time, you don't have hands. The sky is empty. The temperature is invisible. You want familiar, so you imagine a bird. Bowerbird, bowerbird: collector of shiny things. You dream him a tree and soft twigs for a nest. You down cold beer and flip him the bottle caps. The phone rings, you tell him, *wait*."

If you still want to talk about sad things

I'll tell you the story
of the fawn that found me on the roadside
when the gravel was covered with orange leaves
The blackberries we found and ate in fistfuls
when we couldn't sleep How he became
my houseguest and ate through the tablecloth
I'll tell you how the snow came in November
how I scraped it away with a hunter's knife
Pardon my bad table manners
Sorry I'm no good at this What if there
are no new worlds and we jumped into
the water and never came out Our shadows
would lay flat on the river mud And no one
could know who we belonged to

Hands

Eleven is imaginary. See?
Logic isn't fun. Once, as a boy,
a white-gloved magician pulled
a quarter out from behind my ear:
I've been searching for wonder
since. Right now, in Birmingham,
a space botanist waters a fig tree
that is growing in a pressure chamber
replicating Mars's air. The math
states we could live there, plants
could pull light from another
sun to bear fruit to the same
lack of applause. Mouth pulls in,
nose pushes out: two hands reach
to grab a fig out of thin air.

To make winter

* shook the oaks leaf-
bare, * raked the soft
soil, then * planted pine
saplings for *.

Now, we have January forever.

Just like * wanted.

[Result: the river is not a river anymore.

Repetition makes the most brilliant
miracles vanish:

the heart of an ice-trapped frog
waiting to thaw back to life,
ice-coated river weeds warming
in the mouth of a witless goose.]

* want to go there, * want it to be
spring so we can go to the river
and throw smooth rocks
at our reflections, *'d watch
* watch them ripple back
together, then

you'd take my hand
and say something about
starting all over.

Key:
**: you/I /me/we*

Spring Hunters

In a blind, three fat hunters draw straws to see which one will play deer.
This doesn't make any sense to you yet. But it's warm outside again,
and your brothers are getting restless. Mom is still at work like always,
and Dad still hasn't returned from that milk run three months ago.

We can all see where this is heading.

There are only two bows, four boots, and no straws. But this is expected.

Tell yourself this is just boredom.

In the woods, the trees are bare, and the fawn is spotless: meaning helpless

and filthy with mud. In the blind, two hunters flip a quarter to see who gets the first shot.

Your iris needs light to make an image

so it's a shame that material science is the slowest
kind of magic. Right now, in Palo Alto, scientists
are cloning an extinct marsh deer knowing
very well that they don't have the equations
to keep him alive for more than two hours.

They named him *A001.*, giving themselves hundreds
of more tries before having to admit defeat and
move onto B. When you open a math book
you expect problems. When you raise your hand
you expect attention. If you're alone in a white lab
coat in the middle of the night, splicing genes,
you know you have to clap your own hands.

Light reflects off the river and dives into
the eye of a fawn, its shape flipped upside
down and back again before entering its brain.
The unfamiliarity of his own face brings him
to alertness: a car horn blares, he darts away,
knowing fear more than anything else.

An Ars Poetica Where Poems Can't Do Anything

This poem is a trap. As you are trying to understand
the metaphor of it all, the windows are being painted
shut. New notches are hacked into keys. Here's something to keep you
company: you're a five-leaf clover, so no one admires
your brilliance. Now you're Keats, having just dropped out
of med school: the world is yours! You want to write poems
about the trees re-leafing or the moon instructing the tides to eat
the sand of your neighbor's beach house, but there has already
been too much said about that. Since the book about bird calls
is silent, the television is on, even though the African grey parrot can mimic
the sound of keys and can tell its own jokes to pass the time; right now,
while a seagull chokes on a condom wrapper, the robots we built
are building other robots who are not too fond of us. Somewhere else,
at a livestock auction house three cities over from Des Moines,
three businessmen are fixing the prices for broiler chickens, and
there's nothing we can do.

Winter Poem

It's been three weeks since
a sparrow watched her brown,
speckled egg fall to the ground,
and I watched her look away.

*

My reward is at the cove skipping stones
I'll say never found the bedrock.
My reward is jumping
into dime bags without guilt.

Oh, now I'm primal.

Water never freezing, leaves
never turning back into the earth.

Oh, this is how I can love this body.

*

That woman downstream
could be my mother.

*

Guilt: three rocks growing
algae, picking egg yolk off
the hard January soil.

*

The sparrow died for no one,
then I closed my eyes,
and he never died at all.

Dream House #4

The snowman knows
the shortness of February
but finds wonder
thinking about his pebble-
eyes skipping across the
pond. The pond is excited

to be a pond again, to steal
sunrays and hide frog eggs.
Hates its frozen form,
how it stops the hearts
of trout, and humans slip
on its slicked skin.

Just kidding, ponds can't
think, you
warm feather-bodied
creature, flying across the
country. Sunlight seeker,

are you excited
to come home?

At night: maybe sleeping

Some trees are falling,
will fall, have fallen.

There may be many finches
suddenly displaced

without homes. Hopefully,
the trees do not, have not,

will not, land
on anyone's home.

The refrigerator sighs
and takes a break.

However, no chickens have emerged
from their chilled eggs in your house

but, elsewhere, yes,
elsewhere: many chickens, thankfully

none of which see trees
and think *home.*

On the date before the first date

I tell a joke that I read online yesterday, and since we are in Toledo
and this is only our third time meeting,
you laugh.

There really isn't any way
to tell a joke about a feathered
mammal locomoting across the pavement
that isn't darkly ironic or cynical.

Then it's silent.
You smile because it's awkward, I smile because you
are smiling or because I'm actually happy
which means my face would smile.

You tell me that sadness isn't real but sad thoughts are.

I ask you for a sad-thought net and about the ethics of poachers.
You mispronounce a long list of pills that come in many different
colors and shapes but all have the same goal.

I realize you aren't saying their made-up names correctly.
You realize that I'm realizing that you are mispronouncing
those words.

I smile. And your face has the normative reaction to that.

Fuckboy Love Poem

Outside our window,
a bowerbird twists
the green flesh of twig
and weaves it into his nest.
It's almost ready. Reciprocated-
love-seeker, curator of shiny
things.   Close the blinds.
I'm not feeling metaphorical
tonight. Once, I soaked an oxtail
in hot water and lived off
the broth for a week to thin
well. Once, I snorted gas station
pills to get jacked. Obviously,
it didn't work. Take away
the metaphor and what's left
actually happened: loathsome
as   ope, no, no
I mean   just
          could you open
the window? I'll untwist
the paper clips
and he won't have to be alone.

Paranoia/Pronia

There isn't anything more absurd than silence;
when you press a button, you expect action.

So if after you press the button, the button's
action is to drop a gray hummingbird who speaks
perfect Latin onto your shoulder, there's no need
to be grateful.

Okay, great. I'm glad we got that cleared up.

Just to make things more confusing,
there are two buttons. Both red (of course),
and come on, we both know you want to press
one (or both), why are we wasting time:

a single nimbostratus cloud weighing
as much as ten thousand semitrucks
floats above your neck, yet no one is fearful.

Every time a robin crashes into your neighbor's
French doors, it's a conversation piece.
Don't you want to talk about something other
than the weather?

Even in winter, the elms breathe out
exactly what we need. They have come to expect
our poison.

Dress-up

The men in my family tell me
American girls love American boys
in the dark.

I asked my grandfather how to dress.
He wasn't sure what "American boys" wore,
so he dressed me like my brother.

Who wore only polo shirts
and wanted to go to Yale.
He left for New Haven
as I crawled through the spice cabinet.

I can almost smell the ginger root
simmering in the wok. I want to get fat
on white rice and Kalbi,

to hoard each short rib
in the back of my cheek.

As I wait for her, I fill my stomach
with leftover french fries.
I salt each one just to know that it's there.

When she arrives,
I'll ask to keep my shirt on.
What she thinks is more important
than what she sees.

I can picture my childhood bedroom.
The blue-and-red yin-yang flag
hanging from the ceiling. I saw it
every day, so I learned to ignore it.

Relapse Desire #6

Don't trust the cocoon. It's been April
for too long. Look at the clouds,
their shape held hostage by the wind:
a fat boar being stalked down by three
anxious poachers. *No*. Two, bullfrogs
resting in the mud. Now, a fawn,
having seen its own reflection in
the still river for the very first time,
darts off into the sky. *No*. Everything
painted in the absence of gray.

Listen, we can stay here forever, in Tucson.
Rain is a fable, and we don't need
a story to fall asleep. *Forever Awake?*
Yes. Our pillowcases can be day shirts,
and shirt-shirts. *Nightshirts?* Forget
night. Look up: an owl thieves
three robin eggs from the nest,
strong gust, then loses his wings,
but not his feathers. *What about*
our hands? Look at air-space on my two
sides. Did you think "arms"? *No*.
See, the calendar reads October,
and no one is waiting, *Don't you*
want something to be faithful to?

No More Fables on the Third Date

Forgive me, not long ago
I was hiding butter knives in my pillowcase.

Before ground pepper dances on romaine,
she'll ask about my father.

I'll tell her when a father tosses his son
into the air to fall back
into his arms. How a father becomes a god.

I'll leave out scrubbing my cheek-blood
from the sink and the dinner tables
where my mother was left with no one beside her.

Does my date know that boys grow up and fathers grow old?

According to psychology, I'm half my father;
the rest is kissed by lemon rinds and drenched in butter.

Three days ago, I was carving my initials into wine corks.
I haven't slept since.

What else do you want me to believe?

At 7 p.m., the white tablecloths fill with tea lights.
Humor tells me to recite ghost stories.

When I speak softly, I'm asking you to place your eardrum
against my throat.

Cortex fear creeps off my tongue.

What Do You Want to Do Today

On the television: a picture of a boy who has been missing for three days. I ask you what day it is *Thursday* knowing very well that that's not what I meant, but anything is better than *too late*.

*

We are sitting at our table, and the bowls are empty. We are hungry. Does it matter if we have eaten? You pour cereal into the empty space: it's morning or the day has already been too long.

*

Every star already has a tribe
and a pretty name; they call
themselves *Ursa Minor*.

*

We know he's still out there. Left somewhere to go elsewhere.
To be missing from one place while always missing another.

*

The television is not on, so it was my mind. It's morning. So all we have is the past.
Pop quiz: would you rather have hunger or sleep with a pocketknife in your pillowcase?

Answer: you wanted your father's open palm, but every time it was a fist.
Answer: tell your teacher that eye bruise was from T-ball practice.

*

We should be planting trees,
ones with the big leaves that make dark places
for moss to grow. Then he could walk north
and find someplace to mistake for home.

When we make it to the island

there will be no humans left. The horses will have eaten
the leather off each other's backs and forgotten
they were ours. Or remembered

they are horses. Would you swim out to that island
with me? We could both be there. But, if left alone,
we become our past selves

or at least I do:
a mouthful of lime, mangled hair, too-long teeth,
haggling with any god I thought would listen.

How long did I live soaking my stomach lining
with whatever promised to take my body
elsewhere? What was it again that I asked for?

I don't want to be that man again. I won't
be that man again—I will not. But each time
I fold my hands, I find

I'm inside myself again.
Now, I'm the saint,
wondering if there's a prayer
for this or a prayer for that.

Hunger Island

In 100 words or less,
without touching my thinning calves or pinching my sunken cheeks,
prove that we exist.

Don't say anything
about the mango trees: their fruit has been past sweet-rotten for weeks.
The sun says it's August—

noon in every direction,
I rebut: of course the sand has been burning all along!
What was it again,

that saying, about truth:
all the trees are falling, but we take turns closing our eyes.
You hold my face

against your face,
and we try to explain the sounds and the absence of objects.
This is the nonsense we need.

Facing Heritage in the Emergency Room

As my own stomach-blood drips between
my teeth, it's summer everywhere else. The hum of
tube lights takes the world away from a body.

I am asked *Reason for Visit:*
Throwing scissors is harmless. But each blade
comes up bloodstained after passing by the voice box.

Date of Birth:
I'm much too old to be seen as anyone's child.
If I knew my mother,
I'd ask her what to hide from myself.

As for *Gender:*
My hair nearly touches the small of my back.
When I undressed, the nurse saw my bare armpits. My skin too sensitive for roll-on deodorant.
Now, every time the doctors speak of me, they are concerned with pronouns.
I only care about the iron taste that covers my tongue.

Country of Citizenship, Ethnicity:
When I arrived, I was too young to be foreign.
Back home in Seoul, boys must still go to war at eighteen.
Unless they're famous. Olympic medals must hang from their necks.
Not silver. Only gold can save boys from gunshots.
I can't be trusted with my body.

Now at the scale, *Weight, Height:*
In my country of birth, I'd be considered tall.
There's no comparison in the Midwest; I am "too much"
and "not enough" all at once.
This is not supposed to be a problem for men.
Lastly, Insurance, *Consent to Treat:*
They will stitch up my stomach lining and feed me warm Jell-O.
If I speak gently about my history, Medicaid will deem me well.
If you run with scissors, point them inward. Blood from the stomach is richer than any other.

I could bleed out, poor. Or live without worth—no, much worse than that.

Normal Elegy

31/01/2019, Madrid, Spain

The bell tower rang at 9 p.m. in Detroit

the night the bullfighter died; mothers woke
and instructed their children to mourn.

By Tuesday, the note tied to the back of a pigeon arrives
at the cattle rancher's porch

pleading him to raise less aggressive sires.

The channel flows at an unnoticeably
slower pace, the cobblestones don't weather at all,

and a child two towns over wakes
his mother and asks for a piano.

Dream Logic

Typical story: alone on an island. New twist: whatever you dream
will come to life. Wanting company or to dare even *leave* the stagnant sand,
you tell yourself to dream of something useful: the next morning,
you wake to seven flares. For a week, you shoot flares into the air;
no one comes. But each morning, you wake to a new delight:
Monday a bed to sleep in, Tuesday green bananas, Friday a pillow.
By Saturday, already ripe avocados welcome you to the day. As expected,
you are getting arrogant, lonely, and want home. God-like,

with that filthy pride, no crowd to applaud. You want to go home.
So tell yourself to dream of a sailboat and strong winds. Almost home!
You wake and there's a horse mistaking your hair for alfalfa, mistaking
you for his owner, and you know nothing about horses.

So you dream that you've already read through the encyclopedia
labeled *H* and have learned horses don't really like saddles, don't really
need apple-water-soaked bridles to keep them content. Instead
you dream of a water trough and fertile soil to replace the sand. The horse
sleeps open-eyed and standing up, but you already know this has something

to do with fear. New day, no water clinking into the tin. New day, and the
grass seeds stay seeds. He looks at you looking at him, and both of you know
this is no place for a horse. Next day, you wake and the horse is gone.

Assume your dreams were filled with horse-eating creatures. The kind with teeth
that can rip through strong thigh muscles. Maybe wolves, maybe furless tigers—it doesn't matter.
He's not coming back. Or you dreamed of a field with tall grass and wildflowers
in a place where it's always April. You dreamed of other horses, then you dreamed him there.

Two-Year Anniversary

That's interesting
because it is.

And right now, I'm not in the mood
to think about the ramifications of fish being as sentient as dogs.

Before we order, you show me a video on your phone of a salmon
being gored in the eye
with an ice pick on a longshoreman's boat which you claim
is on the coast of Nunavut.

You say they do it this way so the fish
don't tense up and release adrenaline.

I order a salad.
You order your usual.

You turn the sound down because waves are loud,
and fish don't make noise.

I talk about how we are mammals too
and throw our forks on the ground.

You and I skip class for the next day
or three. Your search history shows questions

about boating certification and the collapse of Rome.

All this

for what? Please don't tell me how long
I've spent climbing down the rock-crumbled walls of this mine
hole. Listen, I want to set this pickaxe down as much as you want me
to. But, in the world that we are left in, only diamonds can cut diamonds,
and this faith that we have been shoving between each other's teeth has left
only empty want in all my molar-spaces. Hunger delusion: sometimes in that mine,
I shine the headlight at my face, look back at the vacant diamond-spots
and pretend that the shadow isn't mine. I tell him that he's a good shadow boy,
that he is more than just light and an extension of my own misguided self-devotion.
God, I want more than this hunger-longing. God, I want a mouthful of little, shining Earth-
disasters. God: men have uprooted entire forests, quenched their thirst with calves' blood:
I hack away at the roots of a bramblebush, the dry earth walls fracture. I am wanting an epiphany
but expecting something much worse.

Will you think less

of me when I tell you all my *what-ifs*
are ordinary I've already spent
this month's Powerball winnings
ten times over Big apartment
on the top floor of a tall building
in a big city with fancy restaurants
the kind where I can't pronounce
half the menu so I just order
the Bolognese When I die I want
my body shoved into a space tube
and shot at the sun It's not as expensive
as you would think once you consider
the cost of more traditional options
My grandfather and I went
coffin shopping and he came
to the conclusion that there
is no good way to be dead
so he swore off dying That
was ten years ago and he's kept
that promise ever since
I wouldn't want to go to my own
funeral It would be an odd affair
No coffin No urn Few people
Maybe where my grave
should have been they'd leave a picture
of the Chicago skyline View the penthouse
or even my framed lottery ticket Maybe on
that day when my grandfather is buttoning
his best black shirt after pulling
its wrinkleless form out of a dry-cleaning bag
the scientists in Kazan will have
finally cloned the woolly mammoth
and there will be a video on the news
about the furred boy taking his first steps
that would be something interesting to talk
about over the catered room temperature
pasta salads There's so much out there
that I can't imagine wanting

American Home

In America, the men at work still speak
to my grandfather loud and slow. And he
says the men in his dreams now only speak
American too. He says the sleeping part doesn't
bother him, *dreams aren't supposed to make sense.*
I'm told he has this one dream where, upon landing
on the runway, the airplane's windows break open
and his passport flies into a crow's mouth. In this
same dream, he calls America home: he enrolls
in a night class to learn English so he can talk
about Kobe and Jordan during his lunch break
with his work friends. His daughter doesn't get
teased at school for bringing leftover kimchi jjigae
for lunch. She grows up and has a son who thinks
America is his home too.

Preparations

This morning, you'll wake to the ring of your doorbell, and there will be a box
waiting for you. You haven't ordered anything in weeks. After
examining the box, you'll notice air holes, meaning it's home
to something living.   *Do you feel summoned?*   Maybe it's a bullfrog
resting in displaced river mud. Your kindness creates a new list

of tasks. You go to the pet store to buy another box: this time it's full of feed mice,
who die to please the frog. But he won't eat, and the mice multiply. You build
a rat cage with running tubes and stagnant wheels to pass the time. The frog finds
a path to a river. Now: too many mice and you still with the same dread.
                    You imagine opening a museum of ordinary fears.
A room full of mice, a tall tree to climb, a small windowless room to sit in,
and a fun house with mirrors.   *But who would come?*   It's more
for the adventure, like the road trip movie we rewatch knowing damn well
they never get to Tucson. Don't you want a reason
                              to wake?
There are so many things we should ask for: cribs, car seats, and a spinning mobile
where small furry creatures chase each other's long tails.

You ask me if I like the name Meadow,
and I ask about Clover. Reality doesn't wait for its answer.

Ars Poetica #3

I want to live in the real world.

Where atoms have agreed
upon their organization and
there are more mammals
who eat green plants than mammals
who eat other mammals.

Last weekend at a reading in Long Beach, a famous poet said,
metaphor in poetry is dead!
and then went on to explain how metaphors weaken
both objects they compare.

Example: comparing a lover's face to an August noon.

Answer: what if it's too hot? Or we are in the part
of Alaska where the sun never comes up?

Scientific Answer: There are many studies that *prove*
symmetry is the key factor in facial attractiveness. (Sigh.)

This morning, I looked in the mirror
and withdrew my manuscript
from four different contests.

I want my poems to be about real things.

My poems like real things but only when
they do other real things that they
can't really do.

How long does it take to get a pilot's license?

A Cage in America: Bastard Brothers

Let's eat radish tops and forget our bloodlines.
Now we can set down our sketchbooks and throw out
all the half-drawn pictures of men we hoped
were our fathers. We can finally focus on ourselves.
Rumi says, *the body is what the body does,*
and we've been charging in all the wrong directions:
frying everything in butter, crushing green pills
to sleep, and gladly blaming it all on the men
we could never meet. Listen. In our new
homeland, there are no boys who look like us
and speak "American," and back in Seoul, it's already
tomorrow. Look at me. We were never anyone's
to forget. Here, take this sandpaper: eyebrows fall
into the sink like sickles bullying September maze.

Ordinary Day

I want validation,

so I invite three strangers from the office space
across the parking lot out to lunch.

When I tell them I don't think all dreams have some larger metaphorical meaning,
they timidly nod and then sip their ice water,
stare at the salad section of the menu,
or pick at the table rolls.

I wish I had a third eye so I could pay more attention
to my surroundings.

When I don't sleep well,
I don't bother returning my text messages
because I know I'll be bad company
to my friends.

Jakob has a newborn, and he says
you get used to not sleeping well. He says having something that needs you
has made him more responsible;

he said this while I was retelling the story of that really crazy night
we had in Chicago.

I kind of want to adopt a wallaby,
and I would also like this lunch to be over
so I could go back to work, see my boss,
and quit on the spot.

The five o'clock news is always filled with sad things,
weathermen hedging their bets, and commercials in disguise.

In today's puff piece, the news reporter
is visiting a local bakery that claims to have the best
cherry turnovers on this side of the state.

The reporter asks the baker what his secret is,
the baker replies something about a great
grandmother's recipe,

but I know he really meant, *Help me.*

The Horse Who Licks Mothballs and Swallows Rusty Nails

Don't worry,
the garbage bag in
his stomach is keeping
him safe. Listen,

do you know how hard
it is to use the other side
of a hammer? Useless things:

rubber nails, your self-portrait
etched in white sand, a straw bed
at noon. If papers with nail holes

are blowing in the wind
and the telephone poles
are bare, something *missing*

is becoming *lost.*
The bridle soaked
in apple water. The lead

tied down to nothing.
There's no one left to
stop me from thinking

run. No one to say
the better end of
forgive me. I'm sorry

you stumbled
into this mind.

While You Sleep

In Aurora, a pack of men in cargo shorts
and blazers are conspiring about the future. You are not
one of them. You are a fly resting on the southern
wall of the boardroom, next to the painting of clementines
in a ceramic bowl. The next wall over is a floor-to-ceiling
window; outside that window are other tall buildings
filled with strangers who are also talking about
things that they think are important. To you, little winged
flyer, three-eyed pest, it's all nonsense: scary noise,
just waiting for them to leave their yogurt-ed plates
on the table to spit up on then make your meal.
Maybe it's something about saving the bees
or filling the streets with cars that don't need drivers.
Don't wake yet, I'm still building this day for you.

Acknowledgments

Endless gratitude to the editors of the following journals where many of the poems originally appeared often in different forms:

The Cabinet of Heed, Carve, The Cincinnati Review, The Daily Drunk, Emerge Literary Journal, FERAL: A Journal of Poetry & Art, Frontier, Gordon Square Review, Hampden-Sydney Poetry Review, Hobart, The Journal, Juke Joint, The Lumiere Review, The Margins, The Massachusetts Review, Nashville Review, North Dakota Quarterly, Parentheses Journal, Pleiades, Poetry Online, Portland Review, Rattle, The Rectangle, Re:Locations, and *Salt Hill Journal.*

Photo credit: Danielle Osborn

Sean Cho A. is an MFA candidate and graduate instructor at the University of California Irvine. His work can be found in *The Massachusetts Review, Pleiades, Ninth Letter, Nashville Review,* and *The Penn Review* among others. He volunteers at *Ploughshares, Quarterly West, Button Poetry,* and elsewhere. His scholarly research is interested in the intersections between Asian American diaspora and reader-response theory.

New & Forthcoming Releases

American Home by Sean Cho A.
Winner of the 2020 Autumn House Chapbook Prize, selected by Danusha Laméris

Under the Broom Tree by Natalie Homer

Molly by Kevin Honold
Winner of the 2020 Autumn House Fiction Prize, selected by Dan Chaon

The Animal Indoors by Carly Inghram
Winner of the 2020 CAAPP Book Prize, selected by Terrance Hayes

speculation, n. by Shayla Lawz
Winner of the 2020 Autumn House Poetry Prize, selected by Ilya Kaminsky

All Who Belong May Enter by Nicholas Ward
Winner of the 2020 Autumn House Nonfiction Prize, selected by Jaquira Díaz

The Gardens of Our Childhoods by John Belk
Winner of the 2021 Rising Writer Prize in Poetry, selected by Matthew Dickman

Myth of Pterygium by Diego Gerard Morrison
Winner of the 2021 Rising Writer Prize in Fiction, selected by Maryse Meijer

Out of Order by Alexis Sears
Winner of the 2021 Donald Justice Poetry Prize, selected by Quincy Lehr

Queer Nature: A Poetry Anthology edited by Michael Walsh